I0492269

What you need to know to join a big corporation

By

Clive Verrall

Copyright 2020

Clive Verrall (https://cliveverrall.com/books/)

This ebook is licensed for your personal enjoyment only. This ebook may not be re-sold or given away to other people. If you would like to share this book with another person, please purchase an additional copy for each person. If you're reading this book and did not purchase it, or it was not purchased for your use only, then please return to the website and purchase your own copy. No part of this publication may be reproduced, distributed, or transmitted in any form or by any means, including photocopying, recording, or other electronic or mechanical methods, without the prior written permission of the author, except in the case of brief quotations embodied in critical reviews and certain other non-commercial uses permitted by copyright law. Thank you for respecting the hard work of this author.

Preface

This book is for people with ambition that want to join a big corporation and to make it their career.

Working for a corporation can be very rewarding financially and professionally. You could find yourself working with very bright people from all over the world and gaining experiences that change your perspective on life. Big corporates continue to offer permanent contracts, training, overseas experience and the opportunity to increase your starting compensation 10 times.

Read inside advice on how to find a job with a corporation, what to expect in your first month and how to prepare yourself for a long term career.

This book covers how to join as a:

- Fresh graduate
- Junior (1-2 years)
- Professional

Any previous employment is unlikely to have prepared you for the working culture at a big corporation. A multinational corporation may have more than 200,000 employees globally, with offices in every major city across the world. Its corporate culture is a closed environment with a structure and rules that are not known outside.

There will be a lot to learn to navigate the

organization while at the same time meeting your daily responsibilities. Like you, everyone who joins a major corporation wants to succeed. The rewards are high and so is the competition. The corporations themselves won't teach you how to succeed and therefore the difference between a successful career and a frustrating early departure will depend on how well you can find out this information for yourself. This book will help you.

In this book are key lessons on how to select a corporation, how to get hired and what corporate life will be like when you get there. If you have no work experience, or only have experience in smaller companies then this book will help you close the experience gap and prepare you for a long and successful career.

Once you are employed this book will help answer to questions such as:

- Who is your real boss?
- What to do in your first month?
- How long should you work each day?
- Who to make friends with.

All the explanations in this book come from the practical experiences of real people who have joined corporations and had successful corporate careers spanning twenty to thirty years. I will share years of knowledge, facts, and inside advice with you to help get your corporate career kick-started.

Most career advice in corporate books focuses on choosing the role you want to do (e.g. doctor or lawyer). In my experience, it is equally important to know about the type of organization you are going to work in. This book will help you gain the inside track and boost your career.

Acknowledgments

The author would like to express his gratitude to the following people for spending their time reviewing the book and providing comprehensive feedback. Without their good-will, patience and hard work this book would not be as it is today.

Name	Location
Durga Shanker Pandey	India
Fancois Brault	France
Isaure Venite-Rossi	Canada
James Barker	Thailand
Jatinder Seehra	United Kingdom
Krishna Reddy Vennavaram	India
Paul Simion	Singapore
Renaud de Villemeur	Canada
Shashikant Bhushan	Singapore
Simon Ward	United Kingdom
Sujata Dabhole	United Kingdom

Table of Contents

Make an informed career decision

What is a corporation?

A corporate (or corporation) is a collection of people and assets legally registered to conduct business. The corporation may be private or publicly owned. Most of the big corporates that are the subject of this book, are public corporations which are listed on a public stock exchange. Therefore the shares in these companies are publicly traded. To protect ordinary investors it will have to comply with tight stock exchange regulations on how it does business and how it reports its financial activities. So it is open to scrutiny by those that have invested in it and those who are responsible for its regulation.

The corporation might also be:

- a global corporation
- a multinational corporation
- a global brand

A global corporation has a major presence in every region of the world. This could mean that it has factories, offices, warehouses or any other major real estate in many countries. It would sell into local markets as well as into global wholesale markets. Many of these corporations have a yearly revenue exceeding that of small countries. It is likely to have more than 100,000 employees across the globe. They are a very powerful force in the world. They can be very influential because of the huge number of people that they employ and the number of countries in which they help drive the economy .

A multinational corporation has a local presence in many countries across the world. It can be thought of as being like a global corporation except that it will operate in a carefully chosen selection of countries. It too will be in a very powerful position, particularly in its local markets.

Why work for a corporation?

What can a corporate career offer?

- Long term financial reward
- Unparalleled training opportunities
- Social status
- Worldwide business travel
- Opportunity to work in other countries
- Work with really impressive people
- Fast career growth

A corporation is one of the few organizations that will still offer you a permanent contract. Instead, many organizations only offer fixed-term contracts for no more than 3 years at a time. Although a permanent contract is not a guaranteed job for life, it could last your whole working life. In practical terms, the increased certainty with permanent employment will be a major positive influence if you plan to take out a 25 year home loan.

Taking an alternative career path, a successful entrepreneur could become very rich or could lose their money if the business fails. Working for a corporate offers the opportunity for career growth and improved long term financial reward without taking any risks with your own money. The worst that can happen is that you lose your job and don't earn any more money from your corporate employer.

The Chief Executive Officer (CEO) of a large corporation will earn many millions of dollars every year. You may not aspire to be the CEO with his high profile and stressful role. However, the money trickles down the hierarchy too. So a very senior manager in a large corporation who does not have a public-facing role, could earn more than five hundred thousand dollars per year. The trickle-down continues, and as a result, there are good financial rewards for many people in the company hierarchy.

Working for a corporation that is also a big brand can work wonders for your social status and also help your reputation for career moves you might make later on in life. Imagine if you work in technology and have worked for Google, or your career is in banking and you have worked for Goldman Sachs, or you have decided on a pharmaceuticals career and have worked for GlaxoSmithKline.

Many corporations have offices all over the world. This creates opportunities to visit overseas offices for meetings and short collaborations and also creates opportunities to work at their overseas offices for a few years at a time. Furthermore, if their business is more global than local then these overseas offices will need to work together to deliver the services or products of the company. This creates an opportunity to work with people in many different countries and cultures. When managers are selected in these global organizations then it is a strong advantage if the candidate has experience of working in these different cultures.

The corporation may also own factories or retail outlets. These are out of the scope of this book.

If you worked for a small, low growth organization before joining a corporate then you might have been used to being the smartest person in the room. There is a lot of competition to join good corporates. When you join a large corporate you will regularly meet people that are very bright and productive; and if it is a competitive corporate, with first class rewards, then expect most of your colleagues to be well above the average level of talent found elsewhere.

Many corporations are dynamic places to work. If you can do the job then you are likely to get the job. It is unlikely that you will have to stay in one role for years and years. As a result, a select number of people will rise quickly within the organization. You could be among them.

What compensation can include

There are many different ways in which a corporation may compensate an employee.

- Salary, a fixed amount of money paid monthly
- Bonus, a variable amount paid yearly
- Private pension
- Share options
- Shares

- Private health care

- Private dental care

- Childcare

- Company car

- Company housing

- Reduced cost home loan

- Use of company vacation apartments

- Extended vacation time

- Contribution to good causes

Many organizations may only provide a salary as compensation, others may offer all the types of compensation listed here, and yet another may allow the employee to choose which of the types of compensation he would like within the equivalent total monetary amount.

A corporate private pension could include a guaranteed income at retirement as a fixed percentage of your last salary, a pension where your employer matches every penny in contribution you make to your contribution plan, or a simple private pension that you contribute to each month. Retirement may seem a long way away but the right action early on from your employer could contribute greatly to your financial future.

The number of freelance workers is on the rise. Despite this, remember that all these people working in the "gig" economy will have to organize their own retirement savings plans.

Years ago it was common for big companies to automatically give employees a company car as part of their compensation. This has reduced greatly in recent years as many governments have increased the personal taxes an employee must pay on a company car if they cannot prove that they use it only for company business. An alternative is to offer a car allowance as a cash amount instead of offering a physical car.

Holiday time and vacation allowance can vary widely between corporations. It can be a benefit to receive a longer vacation period from your employer than the industry norm. In some organizations you can "buy" a longer vacation by forgoing a portion of your salary in return for more time off.

A modern benefit that is growing in popularity is where your employer makes a contribution to the charity or community program of your choice. This is usually in the form of giving cash or granting you paid time off to pursue the good cause.

Notice that there is no mention of overtime. The "officers" within a corporation are much more likely to be paid a salary. This means that the employee is expected to work whatever hours are necessary to do their job without further compensation. In practice, it can mean a lot more flexibility than having fixed hours in which to do your work.

There may be other factors that you see as a benefit or at least as a differentiator between organizations. For example, some corporates encourage employees to undergo training sessions throughout the year and you are expected to get involved. Whereas some others see training as a cost or a benefit that needs first to be earned by the employee. Depending on where you are in your career and whether you are good at learning on the job, organized training may be a benefit for you.

Revenue generating roles versus corporate functions

Before applying to a corporate it is important to think whether you want a career in a revenue-generating role or a corporate functions role. This may seem like an oversimplification when there are so many types of jobs but the distinction is enormous and it will be difficult to change track later on in your career.

In a revenue-generating role, the employee makes money for the company or can strongly influence how the business line he is in makes money. In this case, a large part of the employee's compensation is variable and is determined by that person's achievement in generating revenue for the company.

This is unambiguous, the revenue was either generated or it wasn't. The achievement can be measured in terms of a purely monetary amount. There will be no debate as to whether this achievement was to anyone's liking, or whether that person had a complicated private life that year, or even whether the person should be compensated for their achievements in previous years. If they don't meet their revenue targets or they simply don't generate much revenue then their compensation will suffer dramatically.

People in revenue-generating roles accept that not every year will be a good year. Often it can be observed that salespeople (one type of revenue-generating role) move companies before their yearly compensation is reviewed if they already know that they will not meet their targets and therefore they know that their compensation is going to be poor. They may have many reasons for having had a good or a bad year, but they do not doubt as to how that year is going to be measured. If the person in a revenue-generating role has been set performance targets then they also have to live with the added pressure every day of whether they are going to be able to achieve these revenue targets.

Given all of this, why would anyone choose a revenue-generating role?

In a good year when the company makes lots of money and their personal performance is exceptional then they will have a big payday. In some roles, their total compensation could be many multiples of their salary. Furthermore, many people thrive on the excitement and adrenaline of making deals with people and having difficult targets that they need to stretch to reach. For those that don't feel like this then a revenue-generating role could be very stressful.

Another advantage of a revenue generating role is job retention. A revenue generator will be the last person to lose his job in a corporate cost cutting exercise. Of course this only applies to people who are actively generating revenue at the time.

There are also some hybrid role examples. An IT services company, for example, in addition to having high revenue generating salespeople, may also have hybrid roles with a revenue aligned element. A pre-sales IT consultant may receive up to 10% of his total compensation from helping the full time sales people to make sales. It is revenue aligned because if no sales are made then he will not receive any part of his 10% variable pay.

The distinction between revenue generation and corporate function roles affects far more career paths than you may first think. Let's take two examples:

- Law

- IT

If you are a senior manager at a law firm then you will be in a revenue-generating role. However, if a lawyer works for a pharmaceutical company then they would be part of a corporate function supporting the business of the company.

An IT manager at a large retail bank has an important role but his contribution does not immediately impact the revenue of the company, therefore it would be a support function. In comparison, an IT manager that works for an IT services company is likely to have more of an influence over revenue and therefore may be in a revenue-generating role and have revenue targets.

You may well be thinking that there are many non-revenue generating roles in the workplace that don't look at all like corporate functions. An example could be a scientist who is developing a potentially life-saving drug. This work is very important and requires great skill and experience. However, in the world of commerce, it could be said that the development of a drug is a support function. The corporate will then market and sell this drug to generate revenue. The scientist, in this case, is unlikely to have revenue targets.

To help identify the revenue generating roles in an organization, think about where the revenue really comes from in that business. For example, an IT services company typically makes money through sales and therefore their salespeople are the revenue generators not the staff delivering the service. A less obvious example is an Asset Management company, their core business is managing assets but their money is made through the sale of their services and therefore the revenue generators are the sales people and not the asset managers.

Of course there are cases where the sales staff are not the only revenue generators. In an investment bank that sells complex structured derivative products then the specialist derivative lawyers who draw up the product agreements in conjunction with the buyer's lawyers are also considered to be revenue generators.

Remember that in any high margin corporate there will always be more corporate function roles than revenue generators. For example, in big banks, far more people work for functions than in revenue-generating positions.

Remote working

More and more employers, especially since the Covid-19 pandemic, offer the opportunity to work outside the office for some or all of the time. There are advantages for both the employer and the employee. The employer can save on expensive office space while also tapping into a group of potential employees that may otherwise not be attracted to work for this employer. An employee can avoid the commute to work, is less likely to catch a virus while commuting, and may also have increased flexibility about when the work takes place.

Despite this rosy picture, if you consider yourself ambitious in your career then choosing to work remotely could harm your progress. Let me explain why.

When you are a junior in an organization then you will want to learn as much as possible from your colleagues. If you are not in the office then you won't get the same opportunities to get free training from your colleagues. Instead, you will need to identify your weaknesses and formally ask a team member to help you. Also, you won't get to see what other teams or other departments do because any online meetings will only be with your team.

Then when you are looking for your first management opportunity you will have less chance to move to other teams because you won't have had any interaction with them to know what they do and what is on offer. You will also miss out on learning management skills by observation because you won't be in the office to observe other people.

Justifying increases in a compensation review will be more difficult when managers and HR outside your team don't know you and don't know the good work that you have done.

Later on when you want to move internally or leave completely then you won't have had the chance to build up a network of people in the same way as when you regularly meet people at your place of work. Some of these people you meet would leave, join other organizations and then you have an ally in another place. The chances of achieving this as a remote worker are also much lower.

In conclusion, the most ambitious people should opt to spend as much of their working time with other people and that means being in the office (or offices) as often possible. Those who would find that difficult or are slightly less ambitious could consider a hybrid option spending part of their week working remotely.

Must know behavior: Hire and fire

To describe an employer as being a "hire and fire" organization typically means that they vary the number of employees they have depending on where they are in their business cycle. This can mean that when business is good and their revenues are growing then they hire more people. When their revenues start to fall then they reduce the number of employees that they have.

Often it is more complicated than this, a large corporation may have many different lines of business. Each line of business is likely to be independent and therefore one business line might be hiring staff while another business line in the same organization is reducing its staff numbers. Being asked to leave an organization that you have worked hard for and to which you have pinned your career hopes, can be a very emotional time. If the same employer is hiring in other areas while making you redundant then that is likely to hurt.

Employers that have a culture of "hire and fire" may well do it all the time and not just during big changes or due to their business cycles. One example of this is that some corporates aim to drop the bottom 10% of their employees following their yearly appraisals. There are also consultancy companies that insist an employee must know certain subjects by a given date or they will systematically be let go. With these strategies, they are always hiring people and they are nearly always firing someone. Their goal is to get rid of the people that have not performed so that they are continuously striving for the highest productivity and excellence possible within their organization.

If the corporation sees the balance of responsibility is more with the shareholders than with the employees then they may well have a hire and fire policy. The advantage for the employees is that compensation is likely to be higher than normal for that market segment because they are paying for the best people, those that don't reach this level would either have not been offered a job in the first place or they would have left during one of the firing rounds.

Of course, not all organizations are like this, even within the same industry sector. Hire and fire is often associated with American companies because their labor laws offer their employees little protection and they then extend this culture to other countries in which they are operating.

In countries where the labor laws offer more protection to employees then there are less hire and fire organizations. For example, I remember that after the dot com market crashed around 2002 that many banks dramatically reduced their number of employees (especially American banks) and then two years later when the markets improved the same banks recruited more people than they had let go 2 years before. At the same time, friends of mine in European banking organizations didn't witness the same "firing" of staff and employee numbers remained fairly stable. When the markets improved the European organizations didn't need to recruit more people.

Must know behavior: Meritocracy

In the days of gentlemen and old school ties, many people obtained important jobs because of who they were, who they knew, which social class they were and which schools they attended. Then once employed, promotion within the company would have been possible once the person had spent a considerable number of years in their current role. This implied that there was little incentive to work hard aiming for the next rung on the corporate ladder because that hard work would have been misplaced. Also, compensation would have been fixed by the position of their job within the hierarchy and not necessarily linked to their productivity or the value they had generated.

In contrast, an organization that aims to be a meritocracy works very differently. The idea is that each employee has merit and that the position obtained by this person is a direct result of that merit. This starts from the recruitment stage, candidates are only employed if they can demonstrate that they would add value to the organization through their knowledge, skills, talent and hard work. That is to say that they need to demonstrate merit to join the organization, knowing someone or being born into a particular family or having been to a particular university shouldn't make any difference.

Promotions are open to anyone and any new role will be assigned to the person who merits it the most. Ideally, the same organization would be transparent about the opportunities that exist, how to apply for them and then in telling employees who got the job and why.

Corporate compensation in a meritocracy will be directly dependent on the work you have done for the organization, therefore the compensation that your work merits. This is usually achieved by having transparent performance review processes for all employees.

Many corporates aspire to be meritocracies. Unfortunately, many still have a long way to go. Some corporations are too authoritarian to allow merit and transparency to get in the way of the decisions that powerful people want to make. Even in organizations that claim full transparency in advertising and filling roles, senior management can still avoid advertising key roles and instead make private decisions themselves on who should get the role. Whether they make good or bad decisions, it still has the effect of demotivating employees that were expecting a meritocracy.

Entry status and training

There are three general approaches to joining a corporation 1) graduate entry 1) junior entry 1) professional entry

If you have just graduated or are about to graduate then you can consider graduate entry. This includes graduation at all levels, not just for your first degree. Therefore some people who have left industry to do a PhD can consider themselves eligible. This is usually a fast track entry into a corporation and the training will be the best and most comprehensive that they offer.

However, if you are applying one year after graduation then you may not be considered for a graduate entrance anymore at most corporations. Despite this, many corporations regularly hire people at this level and therefore have an established training package to offer. It will not be as extensive as their graduate program because they consider that you already have some experience.

With 2 or more years of experience you will be considered a professional and a corporation will expect you to already be capable of delivering valuable work. Despite this, they may still offer some training when you join that will be specific to their business.

You need to decide which of these you are eligible for. This will help you narrow down the corporations you can apply to. On the whole, I would not give up the opportunity to join a graduate or junior entry program if you are eligible.

Graduate training program

Each company has a different strategy for fresh graduate training. If you join a company as a graduate entrant then you will be obliged to attend whatever form of graduate training program they have organized. Often these courses are designed as a fast track route to a successful career in the company.

Normally there is one graduate training program for the global corporation each year. This means that there will be an opportunity to meet with colleagues from other departments and other countries. In a multinational Corporation of tens of thousands of people, this is a rare opportunity. Many people will find that once they become installed in their department that it is so large and the pressures of work so relentless that they never get to meet anyone else. This leads to a much-polarized view of what the company does and drastically reduces the opportunities for finding a new role.

I know people who joined a multinational Corporation after graduate-entry who complained that 3 years later they hadn't interacted with anyone outside their team and they hadn't met anyone who didn't work on their floor of the building!

The second advantage of the graduate training program is getting to know the star guests that come to talk about their departments. In a big organization, it is rare for junior staff to get to meet the heads of departments or the rising star in a particular area. On the graduate training program these people regularly turn up to share their knowledge, to join graduates for lunch or cocktails after working hours. Even if you are not remembered by the department head at least you will have met him and you will know better what sort of person he is and this may help if you ever need to work with him.

The third advantage of the graduate program is the wide variety of courses that are offered. In many organizations, this can be like taking a mini-MBA. Courses will include what the company does, how it makes money, finance, legal, marketing, deal-making and how to manage clients. Remember that this variety of courses is because one graduate training program is being shared by all departments.

Graduate programs may differ in length. They can vary from one very full week of training to 6 months of classroom training to a yearlong part-time program. The longer programs are often part-time so that the new entrant gets the chance to start their real work, apply what they have learned and then to come back together as a group to learn more and to discuss the real experiences that they have had.

Regardless of the length of the official graduate program, it is also likely that a new graduate will be assigned a mentor that will follow their progress.

Junior professional entry training

Many companies only offer their full graduate training program to graduates within their first year of completing their degree. Despite this, there are still a large number of people who move companies once they have completed one year of employment and found that they have made the wrong choice. These people know what it means to go to work every day but they may be changing careers and therefore still need some training.

These people can still add a lot of value to an organization. Even though they don't get to join the graduate training program many employers offer a special program for them. Typically the program will be short and may only last two weeks. There is still the possibility that they will get a mentor for their first year. Normally these opportunities are not offered to non-graduate hires.

The short training program is likely to be strongly oriented towards the main industry of the corporate that they are joining. Many training sessions from the full graduate training program will not be conducted because it is believed that the new joiners will have had that training with their previous employer.

Professional entry training

When you join as a professional you are expected to be skilled enough to not need any general training such as would be offered to more junior staff that have little work experience.

Your employer may still offer some training automatically when you join. This is particularly likely if they regularly have people join from a different business and it would benefit the organization if they were to learn more about the business of their new employer.

Despite this, if you joined as a professional, it would be a good idea to take some time to settle in and then look to see if there are internal training courses that would help you. When you find some then state your case to your manager.

Applying for corporate work

Where do you want to work?

You will need to decide which country you want to work in. For most people this is easy, they want to work in the country in which they were born, the country in which they grew up and where everyone speaks their language. The community they have around them, their social circle and their family figure highly on their values. For other people this is more complicated, they may have been born in one country, grew up in another country and then went to university in yet another country. Or someone with different ambitions may believe that their prospects are elsewhere and they would like to work in a different place. Therefore, early on you need to decide on the country.

Starting in the 1990s, global corporations were looking for people that they could send to work in one of their branch offices in another country. This was described as expatriation. In the beginning it wasn't popular and therefore to increase the attractiveness it often included a generous overseas allowance and paid housing.

In the present time, employers know that many people want overseas experiences to further their careers so they are less likely today to offer generous expatriation contracts. Therefore many people who want to work overseas for career advantage find that they need to accept the terms and conditions of a local employee in their target country. This could still be very advantageous and is likely to be a life-changing experience in one way or another. Often people from Europe look to spend a few years in Asia or people from Asia spend a few years in Europe. Knowing how your organization works in another country can be a major advantage in a global corporation compared with people who have only ever worked in one country.

Once you have decided on the country then you need to select the city. In some countries, this is easy because there is no more than one hub for your chosen industry. For instance, in the United States, the center for Finance is in New York. In other countries, you may have to visit more than one city before deciding which one to target.

Identifying the right employer for you

What are your values?

If you already know what your values are then the next question is whether your values will only allow you to work for an organization that is aligned with your values or whether that is something you can put aside in the pursuit of your career. This may seem like an odd thing to say. However, if you care about the planet then you will not want to join a corporation that has a record of environmental damage. Sooner or later you will be uncomfortable with what you are being asked to do but you may feel too invested in your current career to be able to change.

A friend once told me he received some honest advice from his manager. He knew that my friend had only been with the global corporation for a few months. He was getting paid a lot more than in his previous employment and this gap was set to increase as he climbed the corporate ladder. Despite this, the demands of the global corporation were significantly higher than at his previous employer. His manager had said to him that he had to decide in the next few months whether he wanted to stay with the global corporation because as the salary gap increased my friend would find it increasingly hard to return to his previous employment even if he had had enough of the global corporation. He risked being caught in a financial trap.

We are all increasingly concerned about the planet, the pollution of our environment, how to live sustainably and what legacy we will leave for future generations. If these are your core values then you can look for corporations for whom their green credentials are important. Many corporations publish a sustainability report along with their annual report. They have extensive Corporate Social Responsibility programs running and they are proud to share information for this on their corporate website.

Think also about how much your values match with hire and fire organizations. If you want to work with the best people possible and you can take the pressure of performing consistently high year after year then this may be for you. Otherwise, you might want to find an organization that has a longer-term view on employment where you can have an "off-year" and people will still value all the good years that you have worked for them.

What stage are you at in your career?

If you are just starting out in your career then you might use different criteria to choose your next employer than if you have 20 years of experience.

When you are starting out then it is most important to move ahead. Few people want to remain in the same role in the first job until they reach retirement. This generally means that you need to join an employer that is successful enough to have an organized approach to careers, that offers training and encourages staff to apply for new positions and to climb the corporate ladder. Most big corporations will do this but you won't find this at small startups.

The power of research

To make a good choice you need to research your prospective employers. Find their website, read about their business, know what their products are and where they do business. Do they have corporate pages on LinkedIn that could give you more information?

Who are the key people at this organization? Who is the CEO? Can you get an idea of the company culture?

Outside of their official websites, search on the internet and on social media. Find out what other people are saying about this employer. Do you know anyone who works there and could give you the inside story (LinkedIn could be a good place to find someone in your network who works there).

Other useful sources of information are salary guideline websites, such as GlassDoor, and company annual reports (not just for financial information but also for an explanation of their current strategy).

Once you know the geographical area and type of role that you are looking for then a useful question to consider is who are the leaders based in that area. The leaders are likely to have the revenue, support and opportunities that you would need.

Keeping track

While you are researching corporates, keep track of what you find. Keep a list of possible employers that you don't want to apply to and write a few words of explanation.

Start your own scorecard for each employer. This is especially useful if you apply to more than one organization at a time. You may find yourself in the lucky position of needing to decide between multiple job offers, keeping track of what you have learned about that employer will help you make the right decision.

Graduate or Junior Entry

Formal Application Process

I suggest using these questions as a checklist to see if you are ready to make applications to employers. Once you know the answers to these questions then you are ready to select employers and to apply to them.

Role required

You need to know exactly the role or list of roles that you want to do. This is a smarter way of asking what you want to do; e.g. to be an engineer or lawyer. Except at this stage, you need to do some research and to find out what the entry-level position would be because this is the actual role that you will be applying for. For example, you may want to be an accountant and the role to apply for at the company could be junior accounts clerk.

Industry sector

Next, it is important to know which industry sector or list of sectors you want to work in. For people in service functions, this possible list of industry sectors could be very wide. An example would be a software developer who could work in almost any industry sector. However, those wanting revenue-generating roles will not have the same freedom as their roles will be more specific to the industry sector.

Desired career path

Think about what your desired career path should be. This may not form part of the application but it needs to be congruent with the role that you apply for and you will probably be asked about this during your interview.

Graduate program offered

Not every organization has an extensive graduate training program and if you are looking to join sometime after graduation then this option may no longer be open to you. You need to decide whether this is important to you or not before selecting employers to apply to. See the earlier section on graduate training for more information.

Your values and their values

List down your values and those that you expect to apply to your career. These can be used as a filter when looking for employers.

Compensation range

If you don't know enough about the employment market to know what your compensation should be for a particular role then at least consider what your minimum compensation level must be to live in the city that you have chosen.

The skills you offer

List down all the skills and advantages you have that would be of benefit to your future employer. Even if these are not part of the application then you will certainly need to explain them during the interview process.

Your CV is complete

Make sure you have a complete and up to date CV ready. Different employers may require you to fill in their detailed forms to provide much the same information, but as long as you have your CV complete then you will have all the information at hand to complete their forms.

Company application research

Major corporations will have a lot of information on their websites about the roles they have to offer and whether they have graduate training programs. Often the only way to apply for their graduate programs is online using the forms on their websites. If a major corporation doesn't have an online application process then it will probably have an application form on its website that can be printed, completed and sent back to them. For these major corporations, you will need to follow their process exactly. Competition will be so high that they will be looking for reasons to reject someone rather than to select them, in which case, making a mistake in their application process will be enough of a reason to reject your application.

Smaller organizations may not have any forms at all and will be more flexible in their application process. In which case it will be necessary to send them your CV and a detailed covering letter including all of the points on the checklist above as well as why you want to work for them and what they should expect from you in return.

The importance of work experience

Work experience can be a real boost towards getting selected for a job or being invited to apply for a job. This should be a two-way evaluation, while you are being sized up by the organization then you should also be thinking whether you want to work for this type of company, this manager, this role, this sector or with these people.

There are many forms of work experience. These could include:

- A summer placement.

- A 3-month placement from college.

- A full year of work experience.

When most people think about work experience then they think about the traditional summer placement. Typically this lasts 4 weeks and is taken between the penultimate and the final years of an undergraduate degree course. This is quite a short period to get to learn any particular role but it is enough for an employer to know whether they would want to work with you on a full-time basis. The advantage to the candidate is that every college and university closes for the summer anyway and therefore everyone is available to apply for a placement regardless of the structure of their course.

Longer work experience is often achieved by choosing a college or university course that has a period of work experience included. These courses are often referred to as thick or thin sandwich placements. A thin sandwich placement usually requires the student to work for an employer in a relevant industry sector for 3 months and a thick sandwich allows for one year of work experience. Typically the education establishment offering the course has links with industry and can help place candidates for their work experience.

Outside of special educational courses, it is possible to gain a full year of work experience by taking a year out before going to college or university. Although it is also common for people to use this time as a gap year to travel and broaden their horizons, it is also a good time to learn more about the career you have in mind by working for a year.

The importance of organized work experience has grown in importance in the last 20 years. I believe that this is because young people are less likely to experience any type of work before they graduate than they were in the past. If someone had worked in a shop or conducted a paper round then it might not have convinced an employer that a candidate would be ideal for their pharmaceutical firm, but they would have known that the person has first-hand experience of what it means to work. They would have learned the discipline of working and they would have some idea of what it would be like to work-for a company. This is less likely to happen now as most countries legislate against young people being in the workforce before their time. Also, the competition to be employed by prestigious corporations has increased so much that they are likely to only accept directly relevant work experience.

A summer placement is best obtained through your networking or by contacting your target employers directly. Ensure that your approach to them is very personal, don't send them all the same standard letter. The letter needs to show that you know something about their company and that you have something to offer them too.

The availability of work experience varies across the world due to differences in culture and employment laws. Opportunities of this kind are less likely to be found in Asia than in Europe or the US.

Graduate Entry Selection

There are many ways to be selected to join a corporation as a graduate. These include.

- Tabletop selection exercises

- Selection days

- Interviews & CVs

- Using an agent

Selection days are where a large number of candidates can be screened in one go, those that pass will have jobs offered to them. The selection days themselves could last anything from half a day to three days depending on the selection exercises that have been planned.

Common selection exercises include character profile tests. These are used to find out what the person is like where the corporation has a clear idea of what types of people it is looking for.

Another common selection test is a multiple-choice logical reasoning test. These tests are intended to require no preparation or background knowledge.

So anyone can take these tests. Those that have the best logical reasoning ability will continue to the next round.

An alternative approach is to test people for their math, English and business knowledge or technical ability. These tests can only be administered if the candidates have attended degree courses that would have helped them build the business knowledge or technical knowledge that they require. It is normally assumed that anyone who has reached degree level should be able to pass the math and English tests.

More thorough selection days could include:

- Making a presentation
- Role play
- Team games
- Psychological evaluation

During any of these selection events, I would expect there to be at least one traditional interview to take place with a human resources expert from the corporation.

A selection day could be conducted without any of these tests or exercises. In which case I would expect there to be multiple rounds of interviews. This normally includes interviews from business line managers, business line staff and also from human resources experts. The business line staff will ask business or technology questions relevant to the experience of the candidate and the role that they are applying for.

The selection days could take place within the corporation's offices, in a hotel, or a third party's office. The days themselves could be run by the HR team from the corporation or they could be subcontracted to a specialist HR outsourcing company.

If there are no selection days then the candidate is likely to face traditional interviews instead of tests and exercises. There is likely to be one interview each time you attend the corporation's offices and then a gap of a few days between each interview. The minimum order of events will be.

1. Domain specific interviews

2. Management interviews

3. HR interviews

A few words of warning about the modern digital world. Most managers, including me, will search for a candidate on the internet while deciding whether to proceed with their application. This is to see if there is any supporting or defamatory information that is easily found about the candidate. So remember, when posting on social media that a post might seem funny now but during the next 30 years every time that you apply for a job someone is going to be looking at that post.

Professional entry

Applying through Recruitment Consultants

A recruitment consultant (or a recruitment agency) will work with many different employers and he will receive a fee for each person finally employed.

Not all recruitment consultants are the same. We can categorize their strategy as being one of these levels of service.

1. Providing lists of possible candidates to the employer with very little research on each candidate.

2. Retained by the employer to fill particular roles in a formal recruitment campaign.

3. Headhunting candidates for a limited number of specific roles.

At the top of this list you find the recruiter is likely to add you easily to his list but there is a high probability that you will be rejected by the employer. At the other end of the scale, you may have to work hard to prove to the recruitment consultant that you are the right person for the role that they are looking to fill. This is because when being paid for headhunting, the recruitment consultant is expected to propose candidates that very closely match the required profile. This requires them to do their screening. If the employer is given candidates that don't match then he will think that his time is being wasted and he will stop using that recruitment consultant.

If you are a professional that wants to leave your current organization and join a corporate then it would be a good idea to prepare your CV and start a conversation with at least one recruitment consultant. Expect to talk to them multiple times and remember that in the beginning, you are assessing their ability to represent you as much as they are assessing where they can place you.

With a good recruitment consultant you should be able to have an open conversation about what type of corporate clients he has (he may not want to tell you the names of his clients at this stage), what type of corporate and what type of role you are looking for and he should be able to tell you whether he can help or not. During this process, he may well propose alternative roles or alternative corporates to the ones you have in mind. His experience will be worth listening to.

You may also be given guidance about your CV. When it comes to writing CVs there is more than one way to tell your story. A good CV is tailored to the job opportunity that you are applying for.

When the recruitment consultant organizes that first appointment for you with a possible employer then expect him to prepare you first. A good recruitment consultant will explain the recruitment process, tell you anything he knows about the people you are going to meet and even share background information that he thinks you should read. When the meeting with the potential employer is over he will contact you to find out how it went. If it doesn't work out then he is likely to propose you as a candidate to other possible employers until either you get a job offer or he decides that you are a bad investment.

I remember the first time a recruitment consultant got me an interview with a major US investment bank. After being given an explanation of the recruitment process and a walk through of the key people that I was likely to meet, then I was given a pack of press cuttings to read. The cuttings included information about the bank itself, its activities in the UK, the products that it sold and some recent gossip. By the time I reached the bank I felt confident that I had really done my research, even though I had simply benefited from a very organized recruitment consultant.

You can expect the recruitment process at the corporate to include multiple interviews. At least one of those interviews will be with your potential line manager and another will be with the Human Resources Department (HR). Depending on the corporate you may also be requested to take some written tests or attend a selection center (a set of tests and interviews with other candidates much like the explanation above for graduate entry).

Responding to job advertisements

If you see a job advertised, or hear that a job is available, then your next point of contact will be with the organization itself. Most likely the contact information given on the advertisement will be for the HR department at that organization or even for a third party (such as a recruitment consultant). In both cases the organization's strategy is for HR or the third party to screen all candidates and only to allow the good candidates to meet the hiring manager (who will eventually become the line manager of the new employee).

Therefore, your goal should be to do everything possible to get through the appointed gatekeeper and to reach the hiring manager. After all, it is only the hiring manager that has the power to hire you.

Use your research skills, personal network and your talent to find out who the hiring manager is. If a recruitment consultant is the gatekeeper, then after an initial discussion they may tell you who the hiring manager is. Otherwise, you will need to find out for yourself.

Once you know who this person is then you can prepare to meet him. Use social media to find out more about him including hobbies, talents, universities attended, career history or anything else that will grab his attention and help you build a connection. You can then either try to contact him directly or at least use the information you now know to slant your CV towards him. In your communication, emphasize the points you now believe will interest him.

Expect there to be multiple interviews before the HR team makes an offer.

Knowing the Human Resources Department

When you work for a company with the size of anything more than 100 people then they are going to have a Human Resources Department (HR) or at least a Human Resources Manager. As far as a candidate applying for a role is concerned or for the employees in the company, the human resources department is the interface between them and the company. Depending on the structure of the organization, the human resources department normally has the following responsibilities.

- Interviewing all external candidates

- Issuing employment contracts

- Issuing expatriation contracts

- Recommending compensation packages

- Setting employee rules and policy

- Managing compensation reviews

- Managing staff appraisals

- Recruiting new staff

- Employee holiday tracking

- Investigating employee grievances

- Terminating employment

- Conducting exit interviews

Therefore when you apply to a corporate your request is typically received by the human resources department and not by the hiring manager. The human resources department will screen the incoming applications, reject the ones that don't fit the agreed company criteria and then ask the hiring manager's team to conduct the first interviews.

Large corporations with lots of staff have large HR departments that are very structured. Depending on the corporation, the HR department may range from a team of people who believe that they only provide a service to the line of business managers or at the other extreme they may believe that they are the core of the corporation. This is significant because it means that the HR team can be very powerful and very influential as to whether someone joins the corporation and whether they then stay for the long term.

In a large corporation expect the HR department to assign representatives for particular staff areas. There is also likely to be a dedicated graduate recruitment team. Similarly, the corporation will assign points of contact for every business line and every department.

One of the key responsibilities of HR is to know the market rate for every role in the organization. They achieve this by buying market salary survey guides from third party research organizations. Typically the third party asks each of its clients to take part in an anonymous salary survey, the anonymous results of which are then shared with the other HR department clients.

As a result, when you apply for a job with a corporate the HR department already knows what they believe their competitors are paying for the same role. Depending on the budget and the strategy of the corporation they may choose to set the compensation for this same role equal to, above or below the market compensation stated in their survey.

How to succeed in your first days at work

First impressions

You will receive a letter from your new employer telling you which of their offices you need to attend on your first day. In the letter, they should also tell you what time to be there and who to meet on arrival.

This may be the first time that you have traveled the route to the office in rush hour. Therefore it is a good idea to plan to arrive early at the office, but don't enter the office any more than 20 minutes early as this makes you look disorganized. So if you arrive very early then find a cafe and have a cup of coffee while

54

you wait.

Be sure that you are dressed correctly for your first day. If the letter doesn't tell you enough about dress requirements then ask their HR team what the dress code is. Remember that many corporates have different dress codes in different buildings (some buildings receive clients and others don't), also the dress code may change depending on the day (e.g. more casual on Friday).

Administrative Work

The very first day working for a company may seem like an anti-climax. Often the day is taken up with HR meetings and administrative activities. You may have filled in several forms before you joined the organization but rarely is this enough. Once you join you could find a whole folder full of new forms to be filled. The forms are likely to cover.

- Bank account details for salary payment

- Pension arrangements, life insurance, etc.

- Signed agreement with company rules and procedures.

- Information on next of kin

Most companies across the world pay their employees electronically. They don't give bank notes in an envelope at the end of the month anymore. They make an electronic transfer of the salary amount directly into the employee's bank account. Some companies are happy to transfer money into an account with any organization that you already bank with. Other companies will insist that you have an account opened with a particular branch of a particular bank before they will make a payment. Normally they have ways to open an account quickly with their preferred bank and this can be useful if you are new to the area or new to the country.

The good news is that you already have a job. The organization has already made its decisions, these additional forms are simply part of the administrative post joining process.

Many companies will also include the following training on the first day

- Building orientation (canteen, meeting rooms, medical facilities, etc)
- IT security
- Data protection
- Anti-corruption
- Compliance (particularly restrictions on share dealing)
- Health and safety at work

The training may be given in several formats from classroom training, to reading booklets or watching a short film. Increasingly, companies need to show proof of having trained the employee and that the employee has reached the necessary standard. Therefore for subjects such as IT security, data protection, anti-corruption, compliance, and health & safety, it is normal to receive a test at the end of the training and to be issued with a certificate if you pass.

With all of these administrative activities complete you will either enter a training program or be shown to your desk and get to meet the team you will be working with.

Before work starts

If you have joined as part of an official graduate or junior training program, then this is the point at which your intensive training will start. It may last anything from a few days to a few weeks, after which you will be allocated your desk.

Getting to your desk

First impressions last. For many people on their first day when they have finished filling in forms then they will get to see their desk and meet the team that they will be working with for the first time. You may have met the manager of the team during your interviews, but it is unlikely that he will have introduced every member of his team until now.

Unless you work for a company that has a strictly open desk policy, which is still rare, then everyone will have their desk and therefore you should have your desk. Don't get fobbed off with being asked to sit at someone else's desk temporarily without being shown where your desk will be. If the company is serious about wanting you to stay for the long term then they will have a desk for you. If no desk is offered and you feel like being flexible then put a time limit on it and make sure you have your own space by the end of the week. Being too flexible at this stage can be seen as a sign of weakness that other people will take advantage of.

The desk you are assigned should be fully equipped and you should have access to a PC or a laptop. If you have been assigned a desk without any equipment then you will be unable to do anything productive, therefore raise this immediately with your manager.

Your manager should take you on a tour and introduce you to everyone in the team. If he doesn't, or at least he doesn't do it immediately, then take the initiative and introduce yourself to those sitting near you in the same block of desks.

Making friends

You may have read in other publications that many people who have worked in a corporate for a long time say that you shouldn't make friends with anyone and that the people you work with are never more than your work colleagues.

I disagree with this approach. We spend the majority of our waking hours at work, to then spend the majority of your working hours without any friends would be soul-destroying. Instead, I advise that you pick your friends wisely. Don't trust everyone and don't become best friends immediately with the first people you meet.

In particular, avoid the office complainer. Do not become close friends with this person or risk being treated yourself with the same negativity.

Who is your real boss?

Early on it is important to understand the structure in which you work. In particular, you will need to know who your boss is and maybe who your client is.

Your real boss is the person who will conduct your yearly career appraisal and will decide on your salary and bonus. Sometimes the person who is introduced to you as your team leader decides what work you are going to do each day but is not the one who is going to conduct your career appraisal or decide on your salary. Alternatively, this person may well conduct your appraisal but does not have the authority to decide your salary or bonus. In each of these cases if the person who was introduced to you as your manager is not going to do all these things then you need to find out who will be doing them and how he will have information to decide if he doesn't manage you directly. There may be no reason for concern but you need to be clear from the beginning.

One such situation like this can occur when your manager is not a permanent employee. In some companies, it is common for team leaders to be contractors but it is against their rules for anyone except a permanent employee to conduct appraisals.

This situation is normally resolved by asking the contractor, who knows your work best, to conduct the appraisal in the presence of his manager and for his manager to sign the appraisal. In that way, you get the right person appraising you and you make sure the information is available "first hand" to the person who decides on your salary and bonus.

Another complication in understanding the structure is whether you are being matrix managed. This occurs often in an organization with a presence in many countries. An employee may have a local manager and also a manager somewhere else in the world. The global manager directs the efforts of all the people that work on his subject wherever they are in the world. Because he is not local to each of these employees he cannot be their direct manager. When it comes to appraisals and compensation discussions he may not influence the local manager. If you think that you might be in this position then you will ask your managers how they will evaluate your performance and which one of them will set your compensation.

If you are in a revenue-generating role then your client will be outside the organization. You need to get to know as much about your client as possible, however, it is not your client that will influence your manager when it comes to your appraisal. Your manager will concentrate on the revenue that you have generated for the corporation that year.

If you are not in a revenue-generating role then your client (or clients) will be other employees of the same organization. You will be providing a service to someone or delivering a product to them. Get to know this client or the person who represents the client if there are many of them. Their input should be included in your appraisal. Many managers will seek their opinion before conducting an appraisal but it is not guaranteed. So you need to know what your client thinks of your work before going into your appraisal.

Once you know who your manager is and if your client is internal to the organization, then you can locate them on the company organization chart. From this, you will be able to see who their bosses are and at what point their management lines join up. If there is ever a dispute then it is this person who is likely to have to adjudicate. You should also get to see how high up in the organization these two people are and how many more people there are between them and the big bosses above them. Knowing this can help you know how best to communicate with them and with what level of detail.

How to fit in

The corporation will have an official dress code written down. Take care to understand what the words in the dress code mean. One of the most problematic phrases is "casual clothes". If the dress code states that casual clothes can be worn on Friday's then what does it mean? Before the first Friday, you need to know if casual clothes mean ripped jeans or smart chinos. Employees who don't meet the criteria are likely to be denied entry to the building by the security guards.

If the dress code is open to interpretation then try to find out what other people intend to wear. What did you see them wearing when they interviewed you? The goal here is not just to meet the minimum requirements of the official dress code but to use your clothes and footwear choices to blend in with your colleagues and to be part of the team. Later on in your career, you might want to stand out from your colleagues but that is not advised when you first join.

Don't just look at the clothes that people wear. Look at their footwear, coats, and jackets too. Look outside of your team and see what people are wearing in your office as a whole. You want to fit in with your team but you don't know if your team is representative of the corporation as a whole.

If you are asked to visit a different office in the first few months of working for the company then it may be a good idea to ask if the dress code is any different at that office. I have seen this happen when front-office and back-office activities were in different offices on a different side of the city. The interpretation of the same official dress code was quite different in both places.

In the early days, it can be very valuable to have lunch with the rest of your team. This is a good way to demonstrate that you do see yourself as being part of the team and that you want to build strong relationships with everyone. After having done this a few times then you can begin to do your own thing at lunchtime if you need to. Depending on how close your team is, you may not get the opportunity to join all of them together for lunch. In which case try to have lunch at least once during the first few weeks with the different clusters of people within the team.

When you first join the corporation you can't know what everyone is like or what other people in the office think about each person. So spend time with all of them. As the weeks go by you might hear rumors or be warned that certain members of your team don't have a good reputation. This can be a difficult situation, you have only recently joined but already you find that the people you are building good relationships with do not have a good reputation across the corporation. You will need to decide at this point on how much this is going to affect your career. If the reputation of any of these people is really bad then as a new joiner with no history to offer people you too could be considered to be like these people. My advice would be to widen your circle of relationships at this point so that you are not seen as only being part of that team.

I remember a case where a senior new joiner regularly had lunch with a colleague who also reported to the same senior manager. The new joiner had heard rumors that the colleague had a reputation for bullying his staff but as peers, they seemed to be getting on OK. After one particular lunchtime, the new joiner was warned by a new friend in another team that many people were noticing who he was having lunch with and he should consider carefully how it looked to be in league with such a bully. The new joiner took the hint and dramatically reduced the number of times he had lunch with this colleague. After another 3 months he learned how bad the reputation of his colleague was and how many senior managers would not accept him to work for them. The new joiner was relieved that he had not got too connected with someone who could well have reduced his opportunities for promotion and left him isolated from the wider community.

Don't behave as though lunchtime is free time. During the working day, there is no such thing as free time. While you are in the building you are being noticed. Instead, make lunch-time an opportunity to build relationships with trustworthy people that will help your career over the long term.

Learn the business language of the organization. Your colleagues will use particular terminology when discussing their work. There may be some three-letter-acronyms (TLAs) that they use regularly. To fit in you need to learn these words and to use them. It is a part of fitting into the culture of the company.

Aim to be efficient

Regardless of how you worked in the past, when you start work at a corporate you need to be efficient. This starts by taking notes of what you need to do. Don't rely on your memory. There will be lots of new things to learn as well as receiving instructions on the tasks that you need to perform. Write them all down.

My personal preference is to keep a ruled line A4 hardback book in which to write all of my notes. If I wrote my notes on loose-leaf sheets of paper then I know that sooner or later I am going to lose some sheets, or they will get out of order and my efficiency and productivity will drop. This is a practice that I have seen many senior managers follow. Even in the age of tablets and smartphones, I haven't seen anyone who can take notes at the speed at which it can be done with paper and pen. Once I have finished with a hardback book then I will ensure the dates of use are written on the spine and then store it with the rest of my notebooks in case I need to go back and refer to it at any point.

It is important to remember what work you need to do and because the work will come from different sources it also needs to be prioritized. This is the purpose of a task list. The list itself should consist of tasks that you have been given by your manager, your clients, from team meetings that you have attended and it should include tasks that you have added yourself when you have reflected on the work you have to do and the responsibilities you need to fulfill for the company.

There are two ways to keep the task list: electronically or on paper. The electronic approach is to use a task application in your smartphone or your email client. Many of these applications are very rich and they make it easy to add special priorities, to add end dates and to sort the tasks quickly. The other approach is to maintain a task list on a sheet of paper, or better still to keep this list in your notebook. The advantage of the paper task list is that it has to be regularly redrawn. This may seem inefficient but in practice I find value in forcing myself to re-read the whole of the current task list, re-prioritize the tasks and then to re-write it cleanly on a new page.

Periodically, re-confirm your task list with your manager or colleagues. You will get rewarded for working on the high priority work and bear in mind that priorities can change.

When you attend team meetings write down anything relevant to you, especially any actions assigned to you. Don't rely on someone else producing meeting minutes that include all the information you need. Some people will write meeting notes that lack the details that you will need, others may take the opportunity to manipulate the situation by writing things that are false or adding actions that were not agreed. To refute the official meeting minutes you will need to have your notes. Once you have attended a few times you may also want to volunteer to take the minutes yourself, this will be good practice for the day when you have management responsibility and it demonstrates that you have the ambition and the capacity to do more. Needless to say, if you write the minutes you can also avoid anyone else manipulating the information.

No-one wants to know that their pet project can't be done. If you are asked to do what seems to be impossible then offer solutions and explain what would need to happen for those solutions to be valid. You don't know if the request is important enough that your conditions will be met. At the very least you will have given a positive answer.

In your first weeks, be careful how quickly you work through your task list. Your future workload may well be based on what your manager remembers from your early days. If you have misunderstood the full scope of a task then you might report that it is finished only to find, when you have learned more about the organization, that there was much more to it.

How long should you work each day?

When you first start working for a corporation, it is difficult to know what time you should arrive in the morning and what time you should leave in the evening. You may have a contract that states categorically that your working day is from 9 am to 5 pm with 30 minutes for lunch. Despite this, I have never heard of a corporation of salaried employees who want to fit in with their team, meet their client's demands and make progress within the organization are ever able to keep to the exact 9 to 5 regime. Remember that if you receive a salary then you are not being paid by the hour.

In Europe, there is a working time directive where employees are protected by the law and do not have to work more than 48 hours in one week. Every major corporation that I know of has a way of asking people to volunteer to opt-out of this directive. That is to say that they are expecting their employees to work more than 48 hours. It would be against the law to penalize an employee for keeping their right to work no more than 48 hours per week but the implication is clear that their career will suffer unless they opt-out.

As a new starter, your best approach to this subject is to watch what the other members of your team do, what time they arrive and what time they leave. Even then, this may not give you a clear answer. Typically you will find early morning people who prefer to be in the office between 7 am and 8 am with the intention to leave early, perhaps even as early as 5 pm. Then there are late morning people who may not even arrive in the office until after the official 9 am start, but they always stay late into the evening (between 7 pm and 8 pm) and therefore no-one takes issue with their late arrival.

Even though I would describe myself as an early morning person, in practice I can see an advantage for the late morning people. Everyone notices that the early morning people leave early but they are not there to see them arrive, so they feel as though the early morning people do a little less than those that stay late. If there is a lot of work to do then psychologically it feels wrong to see early morning people leaving while other people are still working.

An important factor to consider is whether there

are activities that require everyone to be present. For instance, if your manager likes having an early morning meeting at 8 am then everyone needs to be there at that time. Similarly, if you are working very closely with other people in the same team, perhaps paired directly with a colleague, then you will both need to work the same core hours to be efficient.

I heard of a person who was part of a team and he liked to stay and resolve problems after hours. This person would regularly still be at his desk at 9 pm or 10 pm. His working habits evolved from this and he began to stay later and later. Finally, he got to the stage that he would come in late, work through the night and go home just before the rest of the team arrived at 9 am the next day. In the beginning, it was seen as an advantage to the team that someone was able to stay late and fix problems but as time went on they found it increasingly frustrating because they never met to share their plans and priorities. When he unexpectedly worked the night and didn't work during the daytime then he became disconnected from the team. No-one knew what he had done during the night and therefore what they needed to do the next day. As a result of these disagreements, he decided to leave the corporation soon after.

There are many roles in a major corporation where everyone is at their desk before 8 am and they are still there at 8 pm. In which case, there would be no room for early morning or late morning people, everyone would need to be a full day person.

BYOD or Company Equipment

Some corporations will allow you to "Bring Your Own Device" (BYOD) to work. If you really like the special device that you bought yourself, maybe you love a particular brand, then this may sound like a good idea. Before you jump in, you need to know about the paranoia concerning security and privacy that you will encounter in a big corporate.

A lot of their business will be reliant on reputation and trust. If any of their big customers thought that their secret data was accidentally leaked outside the corporate, or that someone was able to change their data without authorization then these customers would take their business elsewhere.

Therefore, a big corporation will want to have total control over the business devices being used. If they do allow BYOD then it will be with very strict rules and it may feel as though you bought a device and have given it to the corporate for their use.

Then there is the subject of productivity. In a big company you will be valued for your contribution. To continue to be valued you need to keep contributing. If you have technical problems then the corporate will want to rebuild your device or give you a replacement device immediately so that you can get back to work. So if you opted for BYOD, you might have no control over your own device being rebuilt by the IT department.

My sincere advice is to let the corporate equip you with their standard company equipment, even if you don't like the brand. Keep a clear dividing line between your own equipment, which you keep at home and use for your own activities, and the company equipment that you only ever use for authorized corporate work.

Why company equipment is no gift

Everyone in a global corporation will need access to technology to do their job. The minimum requirement is that every employee has access to a company PC. Despite the goal of open seating where anyone can sit anywhere, it is most likely that you will have a desk allocated to you and on that desk will be a PC that has been configured for your use. The role that you perform in the company will dictate how powerful the PC needs to be. The PC will be pre-loaded with the applications that you will need to do your job.

There are increasing demands for employees to remain in contact with their work colleagues when they are away from their desk (e.g. in a meeting), outside working hours, during weekends and holidays. To achieve this you may be issued with a company smart-phone and maybe a company laptop or tablet. With these devices, you can be connected 24x7 with your manager, colleagues, and clients.

If you feel the need for some personal downtime then ignoring phone calls or not responding to important emails for hours will be frowned upon by your colleagues. Having been issued with this communications technology it is expected that it is used to the greatest effect. My personal view is that you will need to answer all the phone calls that arrive, whatever time of day or night and you will need to scan your emails regularly. With experience, you will then be able to decide which phone calls and which emails need immediate action and which ones you can explain would be better tackled when you get back into the office the next day.

This company equipment will come with enormous restrictions on how it is used. Major corporations do not issue this equipment to enhance the quality of your personal life, only to enhance your working life and to improve your productivity. Therefore the corporation will want to make sure that nothing interferes with the proper working of this equipment. For these reasons, the company PC, the smartphone, the laptop, and the tablet will all be closed to everything except the corporate network. You will not be able to download new applications onto the smartphone, the USB ports on the laptop, and PC will be disabled and you won't have administration rights on any of these devices. This not only keeps you focused on work but it also reduces the chances of computer viruses entering the corporate network.

The connection between the corporate network and the internet will also be subject to censorship and filtering. The corporation will use a firewall to avoid malicious attacks from the internet coming into the corporate network and it will use the same technology to block the browsing of specific internet sites. This internet browsing censorship can be very extensive. As an example, I was told of a situation where productivity and B2B social media tools (include Wikipedia and LinkedIn) were blocked by a large global corporation that didn't believe that they should be used in the workplace.

These measures are also aimed at protecting the corporation's intellectual property and the privacy of its clients. As a result, it will be near impossible to take electronic files out of the corporation. As stated earlier, the USB ports of the PCs and laptops will be disabled stopping any memory sticks from being used to take data out of the building. The alternative may appear to be to send the data by email. However, not only are all the emails recorded but there is likely to be an automatic trigger on the email system that gets activated every time you try to send an attachment outside. Many corporations have a policy to terminate the employment of anyone caught sending company sensitive material to a third party by email; for the purpose of clarity, your private email hosting company is considered a third party. This action could be taken months after the offense has taken place.

Care must be taken also with corporate email. The email service will be connected to the internet and, except in some extreme cases, it will be possible to send or receive emails from almost anyone. Remember that this is not a substitute for your private email. Every single email that you send or receive will be stored by the corporation for years to come. If ever there is a dispute then the HR department or your manager will be able to read the full history of your emails without needing to ask you first. This happens often and you won't even know. My advice is to write your corporate emails as if you know that a third party is going to read them. This will make you think twice about sending internal or external emails that you later regret.

In my case, for many years I had a personal assistant who had full access to my corporate email. Therefore I very quickly had to get used to the idea that someone was reading all of my corporate email. As a result, I was able to get into the habit of writing emails to one person knowing fully well that they were likely to also be read by completely different people.

There are also legal advantages for the company by locking these devices and storing all messages. If we take an extreme example, the locking of a laptop makes it more difficult to download and store offensive images. Storing all emails would create a complete audit trail of these offensive images being shared amongst employees. Thus, these measures reduce the possibility that the corporation could be considered in any way complicit in this offense.

Your life outside of work

Most of us already have a digital life. We have membership of various social media platforms, we have our public email and perhaps our public website. For all the reasons stated in the previous section, you will not get access to any of these accounts through the equipment issued to you by the corporation. Therefore, if you need to keep in touch during the working day then you will need to bring your own smartphone or tablet into the office every day. It is fairly normal to see people carrying two phones into a meeting, one being their corporate phone and the other being their personal phone.

A more difficult question to answer is how often someone should be using their own devices during the working day. My advice is to use these personal devices in your own time such as during lunch breaks and coffee breaks. Neither your manager nor your colleagues will appreciate someone who is always working on their private projects and not pulling their weight on the real work that they are being paid for. The exception to this could be your personal phone, if you work in an organization where it is acceptable to have your personal phone ring during the day then it would be normal to answer the call efficiently and to postpone any long conversations for another time.

Depending on your role, it is possible that you may not be allowed to use your own laptop or smartphone, even for your own purposes, at any point during the working day. Some offices have secure areas that deal with client sensitive information where the corporate has committed to no leakage of client information. In these situations, you may have to leave your own devices with the security team before entering the secure office space.

If you are involved in brand building of any form for the corporate then you may also have social media accounts for corporate purposes. In this case, your corporate devices will be enabled for these social media accounts only and if you leave the corporation you will have to close these accounts or transfer ownership to another employee.

Many corporations allow their employees time off during the working day to visit the dentist or the doctor. These appointments must always be communicated in advance to your manager. Often the corporation has an online holiday booking system and this is used to request time off to attend doctors' and dentists' appointments too. In this workflow, your manager will have to approve your absence before you take the time off.

When you join a major corporation you might already have a young family, or have responsibilities to your extended family. Despite these responsibilities, it would be rare for a major corporation to allow you time off during the working day regularly to attend to their needs. For instance, I can't think of any example where an employee has been given a blanket agreement to arrive at work late or to leave work early every day to take children to school. In practice, one-off situations can always be discussed directly with your manager and it would be normal for him to be sympathetic even if the request is not strictly part of the official HR policy.

Building security - you are being watched

Outside the offices of the corporation, you will notice that no-one is allowed in without authorization. Normally all employees are issued with electronic access cards that open entry gates allowing one person through at a time. Anyone else has to visit the building reception or the security guard's desk and register before they are allowed into the building.

Once inside the building, the electronic access card is needed to open every door to every room and every corridor. This means that as a permanent employee you need to make sure that you carry your access card with you wherever you go. You won't even be able to visit the restroom and return to your desk without having your access card.

It also means that the security team can identify which room you are in at any point in time. Furthermore, this door activation information is recorded and kept for a long time. HR can investigate where you are spending most of your time, whether you are arriving at work on time and whether you are spending enough hours in the building to meet your contractual commitments.

Add to this that a major corporation will also have surveillance cameras in every office area, lift and corridor and you appreciate that they can construct a complete history of where you were and what you were doing on any given day. Of course, there would be no justification for using these devices to watch employees without any reason. This would prove costly and take up people's time that could be better spent on other activities. The reason for pointing this out is that when you are inside the corporation's buildings it is best to assume that someone is watching, even if they aren't watching now they may well look back at it later on.

Get to know the company rules

Employees lose their jobs very quickly if they break particular company rules. Therefore it is important to understand as early as possible in your employment what the rules are that have high penalties. Every company is different and so it is not possible to include a comprehensive list of all the rules here so instead here are some common areas that you will need to find out more about.

Taking company documents outside the building can lead to termination of employment. As was explained in another chapter, using email to send company documents to a third party can trigger this reaction. Be aware that sending any documents to your home email address will be treated as the same violation of company rules as sending the documents to a true third party.

Consistently arriving late to work without informing your manager in advance can lead to contract termination.

Sharing company information with a third party so that they can profit from it will lead to contract termination. For example, knowing that the company results will be really good that year and telling someone so that they can buy more shares is considered insider trading and will lead to contract termination.

Inaccurately recording the time that you have worked can lead to contract termination. The implication is that the employee has misrepresented his working hours for his gain. Typically this will mean that he has claimed that he started work at 9 am on multiple occasions when he didn't arrive until mid-day. This can become complicated if the employee believes that he was late because he was doing something of benefit for the company; e.g. working from home. This underlines the need to get permission from your manager before doing anything out of the ordinary.

Buying or selling shares for your private benefit without the permission of the corporation can lead to contract termination. This is certainly true for sensitive roles in financial services but it can apply to a large range of other corporations.

I know of a case where someone had been at a big corporation for decades. The rules had changed dramatically since the day he started work and there had been no refresher training. However, when he admitted to trading a few shares on his account without the permission of the corporation then he was treated with no more leniency than someone who had joined that year and who would have had training on the latest share trading policy. He was lucky to get an official warning and to avoid contract termination.

In summary, when you join a corporation, make sure you have access to the official company handbook and read it from cover to cover.

Business trips and off-site corporate events

You should now have the right clothes for attending the office during the week, including any special clothes if there is a casual day.

The next purchasing decisions to consider should include luggage for business trips and corporate events; then casual clothes for corporate events.

Global corporations need to send people overseas quite often. This can be necessary for meeting clients, internal business meetings, industry events, or corporate events. If the corporation has teams of staff all over the world then any corporate event that requires them to come together is going to involve travel.

The minimum that you will require is a solid suitcase on wheels that is just about small enough to store in the overhead locker of a plane if necessary. This could cover both business meetings and corporate event luggage requirements as long as it can hold enough clothes for a week. Find out what clothes are normally worn at corporate events. If the corporation has a casual dress day then the dress requirements for the corporate events may be similar. Even if there is no written dress code, I would still advise dressing conservatively and avoid ripped jeans and t-shirts unless you are clear that this is within the culture of the organization.

If you are sent on a business trip to an office in another country, beware that their personal culture and office culture might be different to what you are used to. Watch carefully and take your lead from your colleagues.

How to spend on business trips

If your work requires you to leave your official place of work and to travel somewhere else then this is classified as being a business trip and you may be entitled to the reimbursement of any (reasonable) expenses that you incur.

Beware that the days of living it up and having a party on company expenses are long gone. Your employer will have a carefully written business trip expense policy which will set out exactly what they will pay for and what your budget is.

You need to find a copy of this policy and read it before spending any money. It is likely to state exactly how much can be spent on each meal and therefore you will need to know this before choosing a restaurant and sitting down to eat.

The policy will also explain which types of expenses will not be paid for by the company. For example, when staying in a hotel, I have never heard of pay-per-view TV channels being paid on expenses. Similarly, many companies will pay for beer with an evening meal but they may not pay for hard liquor.

An important part of the expense policy concerns who you can entertain, how and with how much budget. Typically the only people you can entertain at the company's expense is external clients. The policy in this area is likely to be more generous in terms of budget than if you were dining alone but many restrictions on the type of entertainment are likely to apply.

Big corporates will only allow you to stay in hotels that they have approved. These are hotels that they have agreed preferential rates and bulk discounts with. Normally you won't need to know which hotels these are because your organization will book accommodation for you and their travel team will systematically book the right hotel (or flights) knowing the business you are on and taking into account your seniority within the organization.

Some corporations will issue you with a corporate credit card so that you never have to spend your own money. However, it is becoming increasingly common that you pay for the expense yourself out of your own pocket, after which you then file an expense claim to get your money back from your employer.

Spending more than your budgeted amount on expenses and then trying to claim those expenses will get you noticed for the wrong reasons and is likely to result in you having to pay for those items yourself.

Self-protection

Email has more value than just as a communication mechanism between two people. A frequent use of emails is to record what someone has been asked to do and to communicate with other people in the group that someone is doing their job.

For example, you may be asked to do something with the help of a person in another department and you think there is a risk that this other person won't do as he is being asked. So you may CC your manager on the email request that you send. The email is less likely to be ignored because your manager also has visibility adding weight to the request. Also, if no progress is made, then even months later, you can prove that you did make the request. It may seem like a trivial and bureaucratic thing to do, however, you can bet that your colleagues are doing the same.

Types of people you might meet

Many different types of people work for a corporation. Expect to meet some people that match the fictional profiles in this section. Identifying these traits in the real people at your organization can help you know who can help you and who to avoid.

Clare

She may be on the same team as you. She is friendly and hardworking although she can't understand why after her years in the organization she has not been promoted further. She delivers and is needed in the team.

Clare can help you get your job done. She knows the processes and knows how the company works. Only, be careful when you get promoted instead of her.

Patrick

He is a freelance contractor assigned to the team because there is a restriction on hiring more permanent staff. Unlike everyone else on the team, he chooses to work a strict 9 to 5 schedule as per his contract. He is hardworking and professional but is resented by some of the team members because he works fewer hours than they do and they suspect he is paid more than them too.

Patrick is likely to be someone you can trust and he is not involved in office politics. He knows how to do the job and knows how the same job is done in other organizations. His network inside the company is small but growing; his network outside the company is much larger. It is his network that keeps him employed as a contractor.

Jeremy

Junior manager who sees himself on the fast track to senior management. He has a good education from good institutions and has performed well in his recent positions. He has a lot of self-confidence and doesn't have much time for people he perceives to not be on the same track as him. He is on first-name terms with many people senior to him in the organization.

If he sees that you have the skills to deliver and make him look good as a manager then Jeremy could help you get ahead. Be careful that he may take all the credit for your work.

Bob

He has been passed over for promotion many times. This has left him bitter towards the organization as though he feels they have not delivered on their promises. Most of the time he is low on energy and unmotivated but what he does deliver is OK and every year he continues to hold on to his position.

Bob will help you all the time that he doesn't see you as a threat. He has useful knowledge given the years he has spent working at the corporation. Although, don't expect him to do much for you as he is unmotivated most of the time. Don't get too friendly or else you may also get associated with the negativity from his bitterness.

Stephen

He is a junior member of the team. He is very keen and works all the hours possible, including some weekends without being asked. If he improves his visibility then he may well be a contender for a junior management role otherwise he will give up or burn out. Do not try to compete with the hours he works. He could be a good work colleague.

Elizabeth

Reports directly to senior management with a small team of her own. She is a good talker and very good at communicating up to her bosses. No-one below her in the organization knows what she does for sure but they are careful of her because they know she is listened to by senior management.

Some say that she was once the mistress of a very senior manager, but no-one knows for sure.

Try to keep away from her. She has a lot of useful contacts and information but getting close to her risks tarnishing your reputation or, worse, you may end up doing some of her work to help her look good to senior management.

Mike

A senior manager who expects everyone to use his first name while still acknowledging that he holds a senior position. He is clever but comfortable and doesn't want to take the risk of going too far up the ladder. To maintain his current position he has a very small inner circle of friends, who are the only people he is open with. Although effective, he is a brutal manager who has been known to end the career of many people that have crossed him.

If you accept him as your boss then working for him can be OK. Don't expect high rewards unless you are within his inner circle. Failing to deliver under his management will be a career-ending mistake.

Jean

She is a senior manager that has the respect of many people. Every day she works hard herself even though she is good at delegating and getting the best out of her numerous teams. She can proudly say that she has never held anyone back when a good internal promotion was available to them. She is not small-minded and in all her work she supports the wider objectives of the organization.

This is a good person for an ambitious employee to work for. Expect to be honest and work hard if you are in her team. There will be no room for politics.

Dougal

He is a small team manager whose work life seems to revolve around meetings. Any meeting of any kind (however distantly related to his role) and he will be there. Unfortunately, the value he adds to each meeting is very limited. Despite this, he may send multiple emails about the meeting before and after, usually with his manager in CC of the emails. He can't believe how quickly his diary fills up.

This is not someone that you would want to work for, or someone you would want to aspire to be. Although one way he may be of use to you is if you ever need to know what happened in a particular meeting beyond what was written in the minutes, you can be sure he will have been there in person.

End of month 1 - are you getting what was agreed?

At the end of the first month with the corporation, you need to take stock of what has happened and review whether you received what was promised to you. Remember that in a big organization it is easy for one person to promise something and then to find out later on that they didn't tell the person who needed to make it happen and as a result, it didn't happen. It is unlikely that promises would be made in bad faith but they could easily be forgotten.

The most important point to check is whether you were paid the amount that was agreed. Don't take it for granted that the right amount will have arrived in your bank account by magic. This is the first time that the corporation has tried to pay you. They may not have all the necessary bank account information, the payment may not have been possible but they didn't get round to telling you.

When you have been paid then check the amount that you have received. There are two main reasons for doing this: first of all, you want to check that the amount matches the agreement that you have and secondly this will probably be the first time that you will have seen how much you will receive each month after deductions. During contract discussions the amounts presented would have been the raw amounts before deductions for pension, any extras you opted for, tax and any other government deductions have been taken. Therefore for your budgeting, you need to be sure that you have received the right amount of salary before deductions, that you understand the deductions that have been made and that you know the amount you are then going to receive in your bank account each month.

If you don't believe that your salary or deductions were correct then you need to raise the issue with your HR representative as soon as possible. He will then deal with the problem himself or redirect you to someone in the accounting or payroll department who can deal with your inquiry. If it turns out that a mistake has been made and that you were underpaid then you might find that the corporation is reluctant to correct the problem that day and may ask you to wait until the next month. This is because the corporation has an automated payment system that works on a monthly cycle, it is much easier for them to make a correction that is then implemented in the next automated payroll run than it is to make a manual payment.

Personally, when I have been in this situation I have remained firm and explained that I need the money to pay my bills and that they will be causing me considerable hardship if I have to wait another month. The people who manage the payroll and accounts do not decide your next promotion.

Some time ago an ex-colleague doubled his salary by moving from a small company to a global corporation. He spent lots of money in the first month that he was employed because he believed that his income had dramatically increased and could cover it. When he got paid for the first time at the global corporation he was very disappointed. He had been paid exactly the right amount, but he had not considered the extra tax and other deductions that occurred that month. The amount he received after deductions was much less than twice the amount he was used to receiving. An important lesson had been learned and he spent the next 3 months spending less and paying off his credit card bills.

Was any training promised to you and did it happen in the first month as planned? If it didn't happen then ask your manager, or even the training manager, what date the training will take place. Leave yourself open to the possibility that you had misunderstood that the training would be given.

Were you promised a tour of the building, and did it happen? Perhaps you had received the standard tour but you were waiting to be shown the VIP (top management) areas that are not always accessible. Combined with this could have been the promise of an introduction to certain VIPs. Check with the person who made this promise (probably your manager) and ask when it would be possible to do this. Meeting important people in the organization is always worthwhile and doesn't take much of anyone's time. The benefit to you may not be immediate so be practical about how long it may take to deliver on this promise.

Essential Preparation for the long term

Advancement

Everyone in a corporation wants their career to advance. This can mean many things from climbing the management hierarchy to become recognized as a specialist in your chosen field. For others, job titles or pay are more important measures of advancement.

Remember that to advance you need to be valuable to the company. Advancement normally comes when you have demonstrated that you have the skills to operate at an advanced level and when the corporation has a need for someone to operate at that level.

Think about how you can increase your value to the organization, some examples are:

- International assignment
- Secondment to another department
- Business training
- Management training
- Become a mentor
- Learn a language
- Join an industry group

You also need to be known to have these skills, therefore you need to be visible. Some ways of doing this are:

- Networking with your manager and with other teams
- Volunteer for interdepartmental task forces
- Join corporate social activities
- Over deliver on important tasks

People

Make connections and learn about other people in the organization. This should include:

- Your manager
- Your manager's manager
- Identify allies

- Other teams

- People who are leaving

Your immediate line manager has a lot of influence over what you do today and also over your medium term career. If you have a good working relationship with your manager then it will be easier to understand what he wants and then to meet his expectations. It is not necessary to become the best of friends, but you do need to understand his motivation and his way of working.

The way your manager behaves is influenced by his manager. He has his instructions and he needs to follow them. When you know your manager's manager a little then you may understand better what your manager is asking for. Also, it is important that he can put a face to your name as it will increase confidence when promotions or pay rises are being discussed.

It is not necessary to become friends with everyone. However, it is useful to have some strategically placed allies that can support you. These are people that you know that will at least vouch for you being a good employee and perhaps would be prepared to recommend you to other people. Ideally you will establish allies within your existing management hierarchy (or business line) and outside in other departments.

Don't be surprised to find that some people are

much less productive than you, or that some people seem to have very little to do. It takes many different people to make the culture of big corporations. Remember who these people are, but don't be prejudiced against them in case they become your manager or your colleagues in the future. Strange things can happen in a reorganization.

Conclusion

This book has charted the complete journey from joining a large corporation, that all important first month, rising through the ranks and preparation for the future.

We spend such a large portion of our waking hours at work that it is worth getting the job that you want and making the most of it. Your job should make you happy, leaving you satisfied and fulfilled. A successful career is rarely about just power and money.

I sincerely hope that this book helps you with your career and I wish you all the best for the future.

Clive Verrall

About the Author

Clive Verrall has had a career spanning more than 30 years. During this time he worked in the financial industry for more than 20 years, much of it for a global banking group with more than 200,000 people.

He has lived and worked in 4 countries and traveled for business to more than 20 countries. During his career, he has risen from graduate entry to Chief Operating Officer and every role in between.

At the time of writing, Clive Verrall lives in Asia working on startups that he has invested in and writing books.

When it comes to writing, Clive Verrall specializes in non-fiction, writing about his experiences and those of the people that he has met.

The author can be contacted from his website: (https://cliveverrall.com/contact)

Find out more about the author and his current book projects at (https://cliveverrall.com/books)

Other books by this author

Learn Corporate Culture And Boost Your Career

This book is for people with ambition that want to succeed in the corporate workplace.

Are you making the most of the opportunities available to you? You can see that working for a corporation can be very rewarding financially and professionally for the right people. Do they know something that the rest of the employees don't?

You may have excellent colleagues that can't understand why they haven't had the breaks, while watching other people overtake them. Some people will have plateaued in their career or seem to be out of favor, do you know what happened to them?

In this book are key lessons about corporate life that you can learn now. Aimed at both those people already in the corporate world and those looking to join from smaller organizations. There are detailed explanations of what to expect, which types of people you are likely to meet, navigating company politics, how promotions work and how to survive major changes. Finally, the book explains how you might move on to your next corporate position.

Essential introduction to Investment Banking Information Technology

What do you need to know to become successful in investment banking IT? How does investment banking IT work, what are the essential concepts and the critical IT systems? This book is aimed at anyone in IT who wants to increase their understanding of the rewarding world of investment banking IT. It will be of benefit both to people who know very little about investment banking and want a complete introduction to gain entry and it will also be useful to those who already have experience and want to get a robust understanding of the subject to accelerate their career.

Investment banking is a complicated collection of subjects. It is no surprise that the IT systems built for investment banking can also be complicated and are often implemented only by people who have an in-depth understanding of a particular niche of the investment banking business for which the system is needed. This in-depth knowledge takes years to accumulate and as a result, IT staff with that knowledge are hard to find and are well paid. This makes it difficult for newcomers to break into this large and still growing IT area or even to switch domains within a bank once they have already started. In this book, I will share my experiences gained over more than 20 years to fast track the reader's career.

Throughout the book, investment banking activities are explained in the context of what their demands on the IT department are. For each activity area this includes looking at system diversity, IT team sizes, IT process maturity, technologies used, key IT roles and whether advanced mathematical skills are needed.

Achieve Personal Success in Enterprise IT Offshoring, Outsourcing and Captive Centre Management

You may be involved in offshoring today, your employer may have told you it is planning to offshore or you may have been asked to evaluate a company's strategy which includes offshoring. You may have heard that offshoring saved one organization millions of dollars but simultaneously another organization is mysteriously reducing its outsourcing. But what does it mean and are these subjects comparable?

Offshoring is a huge subject. It has its unique vocabulary and its own set of specific skills that are not part of the mainstream. It has its own models and life cycles. It is a product of the "flat world" and the interconnected global economy that we now live in. If you want to understand the practicalities of this subject to ensure your personal success in offshoring, outsourcing, building an offshore center, or in setting IT strategy or you are just curious about lifting the lid on this vast subject then this book will help you.

The book focuses on the offshoring of IT activities from corporate IT departments to their offshore facilities or an outsourcing vendor. It will also give examples of how this extends to cover non-IT Business Process Offshoring activities. This book includes advice and lessons learned from real offshoring experiences. This is not a book about statistical trends in offshoring or untested management theory.

Raising your internet business: How to deliver successful web projects for your small business

Do you want your business to be among many businesses that thrive and expand due to their successful online business models? Many of these businesses derive the majority of their revenues from internet customers whom the businesses will never meet, or from customers who find the businesses online and then visit the businesses' physical premises.

How do these businesses attract these customers? These opportunities are only possible if your business has an online presence. How do I put my business online? What services should I offer? How will I accomplish all of this on a small business budget? You may have a vision of the website you would like to have, but as a small business owner, you probably won't have an IT department to which you can delegate this project responsibility. You can hire experts to help you, but you won't know how to supervise them unless you first gain an understanding of the key subjects involved. How can you negotiate a good deal unless you already know the advantages and pitfalls of putting your business online?

As a web professional, I have regularly been asked these questions by my myriad clients. Usually, I only have time to give clients a quick answer, and not enough time to explain everything I'd like. This book contains the more comprehensive answers that I would like to have told my clients, and from which any small business reader can now benefit.

Put all these explanations together, and this book gives you the essential information you need to get your business online.

Visit (https://cliveverrall.com/books/) to find out more.

www.ingramcontent.com/pod-product-compliance
Lightning Source LLC
Chambersburg PA
CBHW070611220526
45467CB00003B/1383